SPEED

2.44
W13

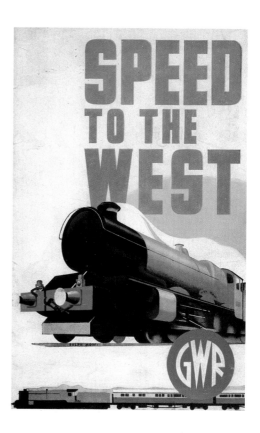

Aldo Delicata and Beverley Cole

Capital Transport

First published 2000

ISBN 185414 228 3

Published in association with the
National Railway Museum by
Capital Transport Publishing,
38 Long Elmes, Harrow Weald,
Middlesex

Printed by CS Graphics, Singapore

The posters in this book are from the collection of the
National Railway Museum, and most of the publicity items
from the collections of Aldo Delicata and R. King Bird.
We are also grateful to the Great Western Trust and to
Stan Friedman.

Introduction

On the first of January 1923, all the main line railways in Britain were amalgamated to form four companies, the Great Western Railway, the London, Midland and Scottish Railway, the London and North Eastern Railway and the Southern Railway.

The GWR was unique in as much that it was the only company to retain its original title from formation in 1835 until Nationalisation in 1948, a period of 112 years.

Publicity in the form of letterpress posters, handbills and timetables exists from the very early days, but it was not until the Inter-war years that illustrated covers became the accepted practice, many designed by prominent artists of the day such as Charles Mayo and Frank Newbould.

The peak period of GWR publicity during the 1930s produced some superb designs and artwork. This booklet covers the period from Amalgamation to Nationalisation, with brief reference to other forms of publicity produced by the company.

The GWR was fortunate that its publicity department was not greatly disrupted by the Amalgamation, and the smaller absorbed railways were to have little effect on its output although the Cambrian Railway did cover much of the west coast of Wales, and the Barry Railway had the popular resort of Barry Island on its system.

Prior to this time however, advertising and publicity appears to have been of only secondary importance to the company, and it was not until 1886 that a proper advertising department was formed with a few clerks and even fewer directives!

In the 1890s a London publisher named Walter Hill produced a series of booklets for several railway companies giving details of hotels and resorts, with the GWR version appearing in 1894 and then regularly until 1905.

James C. Inglis (1851–1911) became General Manager in 1904 and had much influence on the publicity of the day. Felix Pole (1877–1956) and W.H. Fraser built on these foundations after World War I. When Fraser retired in 1931, K.W.C. Grand (1900–1983), who had been the GWR general agent in USA and Canada and Fraser's assistant, became the first head of the advertising department up to (and beyond) Nationalisation in 1948. The items illustrated in this book were produced during the period between 1923 and 1948.

The earliest GWR posters followed the same style as handbills and timetables, being printed in letterpress, and remained this way until pictorial versions began to appear in the latter part of the nineteenth century.

Cover of a 1927 booklet aimed at the American tourist market.

Cover from a series of booklets published by the GWR to promote the attractions of a winter holiday in Devon, Cornwall and other places served by the company. 'The question then is not so much shall we winter in the West as where shall we winter in the West? There is such an embarrassment of riches, that this is not easy to answer,' reflected this 1933 guide.

The oldest surviving illustrated poster 'The Ascot Races' dated June 1897 is preserved in the GWR Museum at Swindon. An even older example dated 1889 for the 'Royal Tournament' also survives in letterpress form with a coloured lithograph as a centrepiece.

Various very colourful posters were produced prior to 1914, being the responsibility of one Alec Fraser, and covered the usual subjects of Devon, Cornwall, North Wales, the Thames Valley, etc, but the designs were considered to be over fussy and cluttered.

There was initially little improvement after the war although Felix Pole sponsored a competition for poster designs. This was not a success, and other railways, particularly the London Underground, began commissioning well established artists of the day to produce superior designs.

Fred Taylor, a leading poster artist of his time, was asked to produce several posters for the GWR including 'Exeter Cathedral' (1926) – this was later used as an illustration for a jigsaw puzzle.

Many pictorial posters around this period were joint designs issued in co-operation with town tourist offices, who shared the costs with the railway, and used the talents of artists including Frank Newbould, Claude Buckle, Ronald Lampitt and Charles Mayo (the last named actually worked in the publicity department after transferring from the traffic side). The illustrations signed 'Ralph Mott' were produced by various artists working for 'Ralph and Mott', a firm of artists' agents, and therefore most remained anonymous.

The peak of poster production was reached in the mid 1930s, and this also applied to guides and booklets produced by the GWR. With the advent of the car and alternative forms of transport after the Second World War, the demand for colourful advertising on the railway slowly declined and was never quite the same again.

A 1937 booklet giving details of combined railway and motor coach tours of places of interest.

SPEED TO THE WEST

CORNWALL DEVON SOMERSET WALES

6

Speed to the West by Chas Mayo, 1939 (*left*)
This was the most successful poster the GWR
produced in the late 1930s when the steam
locomotive was in its heyday. Charles Mayo, the
artist, worked in the publicity department of the GWR
and produced artwork for posters, booklets and other
publicity material. Here we see a 'King' class
locomotive pulling a holiday train destined for the
West Country. The GWR also published a book about
these locomotives with the title 'The King of Railway
Locomotives'. It was the fourth volume in a series
'for boys of all ages' and, like the others, was the
work of W.G. Chapman. It began with a quote from
the *New York Herald Tribune*:
'Somewhere in the breast of every normal homo
sapiens there stretches a chord which vibrates only
to the sight of a fine locomotive. Even now, with
airplanes and motors to bid against it in its own
field of romantic interest, the steam locomotive
retains its fascination'. The poster was also
published for display in the USA with the words
'The Great Western Railway of England' added
and the names of the counties omitted. It was
reprinted in Britain in 1946 without the black line
at the bottom. In 1939 2,500 were printed for the
British market and 500 for the USA.

'Speed to the West'
was also the title of this simplified booklet (1939) of only
16 pages listing resorts and quiet retreats in the West Country and Wales with
a few illustrations, sketch map of the railway, and a list of specimen third class
monthly return fares. An additional note stated that first class tickets were
approximately 50% higher in price compared with the third class fares shown.
'Not only in summer but all the year round the glorious West Country calls
invitingly to the city worker, bidding him come away, if only for a few days, to
find rest and quiet, health and pleasure, in this enchanting countryside.'

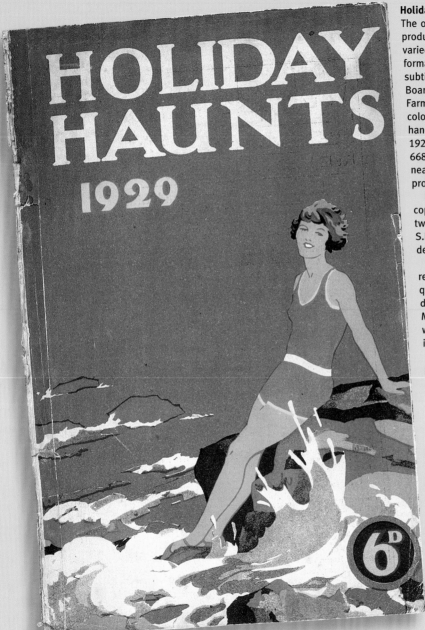

HOLIDAY HAUNTS
1929
6D

Holiday Haunts

The original editions of 'Holiday Haunts' were produced with a not unattractive titled cover which varied with each issue until 1911 when a 'standard' format was adopted with title, season, and date, subtitled 'Health and Pleasure Resorts, Hotels, Boarding Houses, Seaside and Country Lodgings, Farmhouses'. The covers were of thin card, usually coloured, with the company crest at the top right hand side, and this remained unchanged up to 1928. The first issue had 334 pages, increasing to 668 pages in 1911 and 1914, with a circulation of nearly 100,000 copies. A separate section was also produced for Southern Ireland.

By the last issue in this format, some 200,000 copies were printed, but with the appearance of two travel books written for the company by S.P.B. Mais bearing attractive covers, it was decided to revamp the guides.

Consequently the 1929 edition appeared with a red costumed bathing beauty adorning its cover, quite a contrast to previous editions, and the design was changed every year from then on. Miss Maxwell Fraser, daughter of W.H. Fraser, was responsible for this and all subsequent issues.

The 1935 'GWR Centenary' number was printed in the 'house colours' of chocolate and cream, and by 1937 (Coronation Year), the guides had reached over 1,000 pages.

All the 'Holiday Haunts' were made available in hardback form, some even finding their way onto cruise ships with the name of the ship embossed in gold on the cover, together with other publications of the company bound in similar style.

HOLIDAY HAUNTS 1933

1934 GWR HOLIDAY HAUNTS ~ 6D.

When hostilities commenced in 1939, the next year's issue was already in production, so it was decided to go ahead with a somewhat smaller edition of 744 pages using a plain half tone illustration on the cover. Needless to say, much that was on offer in this guide became unavailable due to prevailing conditions. No further guides were produced until after the war. The 1947 edition became the 32nd and last to appear – with Nationalisation looming the 'writing was on the wall'.

Issued concurrently with 'Holiday Haunts', the booklet 'Holidays' was a simplified version giving basic details of locations on the GWR system. Each was illustrated, but lacked any accommodation addresses and advertising apart from listing company publications, services and offices and agencies in London and the Provinces. The standard system map was still included, as with so many other guides. The two examples illustrated date from 1931 and 1932.

Somerset by Frank Newbould, 1936; **Devon** by Frank Newbould, 1936

These are two of a series of three advertising counties to visit in the West Country. The missing one is Cornwall. 3,000 of each were printed and the artist was paid £114 17s 6d for all three designs.

Somerset was advertised as a land of pleasant valleys, sprinkled with 'olde world' villages and blessed with a happy, comfortable atmosphere and a land of peace and stillness. Devon, often described as glorious, was blessed with the amenities of the seaside and beautiful scenery in both its coast and moors. It also called itself 'The lovely land of the *Mayflower*' to attract American visitors. In 1620 the pilgrim fathers sailed from Plymouth UK on the *Mayflower* to 'New Plymouth' in the USA.

Frank Newbould was a prolific poster designer who worked for all of the big four railway companies as well as the Orient Line and Belgian railways. In 1942 he joined the War Office working as an assistant to Abram Games. Newbould claimed to have started a landscape school in British Poster design.

Cornwall by Edward McKnight Kauffer, 1933

This is one of a series of six posters featuring Devon and Cornwall. McKnight Kauffer was influenced by the new European art movements of the early twentieth century and had established his reputation with his work for London Transport. His designs made great use of geometrical patterns. 2,000 copies of each poster were printed. The others in the series were 'St Ives', 'Sunset', 'Lanes', 'Yachts' and 'Dartmoor'. The artist was paid £314 10s for the series.

'Somerset' has more varied scenery than any other county, covering an area from Clevedon to Minehead, Wells and Taunton down to Chard, Cheddar and Glastonbury, offering a wealth of places to visit for the traveller on the GWR. Villages, churches, wooded hills, country cottages and seaside are on offer, not forgetting hunting on Exmoor and many historical sites.

These three guides (1937–39) all advertise 'Holiday Haunts' and 'Somerset' (both by Maxwell Fraser). It is interesting to see the contrasting styles of artwork over the three consecutive years.

Devon, sometimes mispronounced 'Heaven', and described as 'vivid, and so intensely alive in its beauty'. As with Somerset, the GWR was fortunate to have so much to offer its passengers, even to the point of describing its winters as more equable than many famous Mediterranean resorts. 'An overcoat is a superfluity on nine days out of ten.' Its seaside resorts were obviously its forte, but it also had rivers and moors to offer. The two coastlines were nearly 100 miles long and less than 50 miles apart, giving much choice of destination to the traveller. These two guides date from 1932 and 1937.

Cornish miners and Cornish pasties, tin and china clay were hardly the best things to offer the holidaymaker to this area, but gigantic cliffs, sheltered sandy beaches, quaint villages and the glamour of Cornish legends and history (not forgetting the clotted cream teas) helped to sway the balance. Evocative names such as Mousehole, St Michaels Mount and Tintagel (for King Arthur and the Round Table) come to mind (1937 and 1938). Between the years 1923 and 1948 the GWR owned eight hotels including the 'Royal' at Paddington, the Fishguard Bay Hotel, the Manor House Hotel at Moretonhampstead, and the Tregenna Castle Hotel overlooking St Ives, some of which still exist today under private ownership.

The luggage label illustrated is from the Tregenna Castle Hotel, which was leased by the GWR in 1878 but dates from 1774, and resembles a real castle with its crenellated stonework. The hotel was purchased outright in 1895. It was extended between the wars, a golf course was laid, and it had its own farm which built up a reputation in the area for winning prizes at cattle and agriculture shows. It was transferred to the British Transport Commission Hotels in 1948, sold to private owners in 1983 and is still open, although little remains today to identify its previous owners.

The 1938 guide illustrated here suggesting that you 'Settle for a while in bright spots' was intended to encourage the early season traveller to visit the West Country or Wales during the Easter or Whitsun breaks.

Offering a thousand miles of coast from Weymouth to Pwllheli, the great triangle of territory contained an infinite variety of moorlands, wooded valleys, bathing coves, delightful little hamlets and splendid seaside resorts, citing the immense health value of an early holiday, not to mention less crowds and cheaper accommodation, etc. Each section of the guide lists 'bright spots and quiet retreats' for the traveller.

Somerset by Maxwell Fraser (1934).
'Miss Fraser describes the scenery delightfully and there are very many historical and interesting facts to be found in this book', ran the advert. One of the most popular GWR guides, it was produced as a companion to 'Glorious Devon'. Intended to be around 15,000 words, Miss Fraser had so much to say about her favourite county that the final product more than doubled the number of words. Apparently the publicity agent of the time, K.W.C. Grand, was so impressed that it was published in full. Two editions plus a hardback version were produced.

Glorious Devon by S.P.B. Mais (1928). Having just completed a book for the Southern Railway called 'My Finest Holiday', Mr Mais was requested to write a guide book on Devon in conjunction with a similar book to be called 'The Cornish Riviera'. They proved so popular that the original print run of 10,000 copies of each book were soon exhausted and new editions were quickly produced in time for the following season. The illustration comes from the 3rd edition of 1934.

The Torbay Limited or Torbay Express luggage label. The 12 noon departure from Paddington to Torquay took 3½ hours to complete its journey with a five minute stop at Exeter, reaching Kingswear at an average speed of 60mph. The train was unusual in that the down and up journeys both departed at the same time.

Torquay (1936).

'It is curiously appropriate that Torquay should be the only English resort which can boast the praise of the Emperor Napoleon'. This was the introduction to the guide giving the usual details and illustrations of the facilities on offer. 'Torquay is a town of many climates, enabling the best use to be made of its various amenities, for it is built on the sides and at the foot of its seven hills and covers a wide area – to catch sea breezes whichever way they blow!'

Torquay was promoted as the capital of the 'English Riviera'. The climate was so mild that palm trees and exotic flowers flourished.

S.P.B. Mais, in 1934, described this resort: 'Torquay unveils her beauties very gradually. It is not from the railway, which is tucked away unobtrusively, that her peculiar glories are to be seen. Each separate area of beauty is self contained and individual. Here is no hard glittering ruler-line of a grand promenade, going endlessly, tirelessly on until it emerges into the grander, no-less-straight and tiring promenade of the next resort. Instead of that, you find yourself cleft of a vast bay, where you may see without being seen.'

The publicity department also claimed that 'the sole industry of Torquay is the manufacture of health'.

Three illustrated guides from 1935–38 covering Exeter, Plymouth, Dartmouth, Torquay, Paignton, etc, including Exmouth (via the Southern Railway), with brief descriptions of facilities. The text from one of the guides rather sums up the area: 'It is not only in its infinite variety but also in the wonderful equability of its climate that the secret of South Devon's popularity most surely lies, for its resorts are not simply places where an enjoyable summer holiday may be spent, but where, at all periods of the year, a short visit or lengthy residence is thoroughly beneficial'.

1936

April 1935

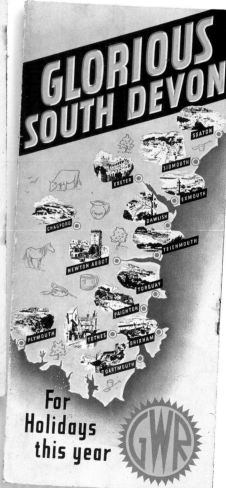

1938 Season

Paignton by Chas Pears, 1938.
Paignton was famous for its long sandy beach and the GWR has used this to appeal to families on this poster. By this time improvements in the standard of living for most people meant that families had more money to spend on leisure. An increasing number of Britain's workforce enjoyed paid holidays and it was this market the GWR was targeting with its seaside holiday posters. This bright cheery design offered escapism for a week from the mundane day to day routine.

The artist, Chas Pears began his career as a marine painter and then during the First and Second World Wars he was an official naval artist. He also designed posters for all the 'big 4' railway companies and the Empire Marketing Board. His poster designs were such that designs of 'Gibraltar' and 'Paignton' were almost interchangeable.

1930

September 1933

Winter Resorts.

To encourage further use of the railway out of season, the publicity department produced literature extolling the virtues of holidays or short breaks, suggesting that the public tended to be 'in a groove' by accepting August as its holiday month, forgetting the fact that it is often the wettest period of the year.

There was much to offer in Torquay, Falmouth and Weston-super-Mare, plus the coastal scenery of Devon, Cornwall and Wales.

The usual advantages were listed. There were fewer crowds, and the weather was more suitable for walking or playing golf, combined with the warmth of central heating and log fires in the evenings, perhaps with a game of billiards or bridge in the hotel (of which many were plying for business). These booklets were all written by S.P.B. Mais or Maxwell Fraser and issued between 1930 and 1935. The 1933 edition optimistically illustrates a couple under a sunshade!

1935

1937

1938

By way of contrast, the GWR offered passengers a selection of inland destinations on its system, including the Wye Valley (1937), which went from Chepstow to Ross via Tintern and Monmouth. Herefordshire has no less than 60 miles of the River Wye, the beauty of which culminates in the enchanting Symonds Yat.

In similar vein, but covering the area of the Cotswolds and Malvern Hills, the Mendips and the Quantocks, the guides entitled 'Western Hills and Moorlands' (1935–38) offered many tours for ramblers with districts of unspoilt natural scenery, the railway and motor bus services being sufficiently close to avoid unprofitable walking at the outset. Doctor Beeching was obviously not a rambler!

1935

Spring
1937

The Isles of Scilly.

Various folding guides were produced between 1935 and 1939 with daffodils as the main theme. The Scilly Isles have been described as having only two seasons, spring and summer, and there are very few weeks in the year when the islands cannot offer visitors some new and delightful experience.

In 1934, well over 1,000 tons of flowers were shipped to the mainland, and at the height of the season as many as a million and a half daffodils were picked in a day!

Visitors travelled from Penzance via the R.M.S. *Scillonian* (subject to weather) at around 9.30 am, with the return scheduled to depart at 4.15 pm. Cheap day trips were encouraged at 10s return, with weekend visits (Saturday to Monday), or any two weekdays at 12s 6d. At Penzance, the harbour was located most conveniently adjacent to the GWR station.

Spring
1937

Spring
1939

The Ocean Coast (1931).
The Ocean Coast stretches from Dorset to North Wales – 1,000 miles of ever varying scenery from the gaiety of large towns or the peace of tiny hamlets, magnificent bathing beaches, rock strewn shores, gigantic cliffs or breezy downs. Most of the places listed were directly affected by the Gulf Stream, with its warm, ozone-laden breezes.

The Malverns (1931).
This guide gave details of the three week Festival during August held in Malvern covering five centuries of English drama, with plays and lectures. The railway offered special cheap tickets to this event.

Wookey Hole Caves and Wells (1936).
This version offered inclusive fares to both these places with special excursions from Paddington via Bath on certain Sundays at a return fare of 10s. 'No caves yet discovered in England have the charm or human interest to the same degree as the caverns of Wookey Hole!'

Not short on superlatives, the publicity department latched onto the 'Glorious' theme, as these three guides show. The 'Glorious West' (1934), 'South Devon' and 'Thames' (1935) were produced with the usual inside format of black and white illustrations and text. The introduction to the latter sums up the style of presentation: 'We will go along the Thames, watch the water flow unhurriedly by, explore backwaters where the only movement is the shimmer of the heat and the only sound the soft drone of bees'. Many larger stations and agents put various guides similar to these on display in custom made wooden racks with the logo 'GWR Publications – Please Take One' painted in gold letters.

This 'matching' 1936 group covering
virtually all of the GWR West of
England and Wales was produced
with the now accepted style as
used in the 'Glorious' series.
Further editions were also available
for the Isle of Man (via Birkenhead
or Liverpool) and Southern Ireland
(via Fishguard).

DEVON

CHEDDAR, WELLS & GLASTONBURY

WALES

GWR

GWR

GWR

Wales

A range of colourful guides to Wales was produced from 1931 to 1938 including artwork attributed to 'Ralph Mott'. Ralph & Mott was a firm of artists' agents. They employed a team of artists whose work can be found on many Great Western posters under the pseudonym Ralph Mott. Some of the artists became well known in their own right in later years. Much of the territory covered in these leaflets originally belonged to the old Cambrian Railways from Aberystwyth to Pwllheli, but Carmarthan to Fishguard and Cardigan are also mentioned. Holiday tickets were available giving weekly unlimited travel within the areas specified. The lady in traditional dress seems to have been obligatory on each cover with the exception of 'Wales For Lovely Scenery' by Maxwell Fraser (1932), which was produced for the American market.

CADER IDRIS & THE AFON MAWDDACH

 WALES

G.W.R. PADDINGTON STATION, LONDON, W.2.   PRINTED IN GREAT BRITAIN BY LOWE & BRYDONE PRINTERS LTD, LONDON, N.W.10.   JAMES MILNE, GENERAL MANAGER

Wales – Cader Idris and the Afon Mawddach by H. Alker Tripp, 1937.
Cader Idris is a mountain towering over the Mawdacch estuary and now part of the Snowdonia National Park. It is ten miles long by 3 miles wide and is 2,929 feet at its highest. Idris was the legendary King Arthur, who was reputed to have been in Wales in the sixth century. The artist, Sir Herbert Alker Tripp had a long and successful career as a detective with New Scotland Yard, painting only in his spare time.

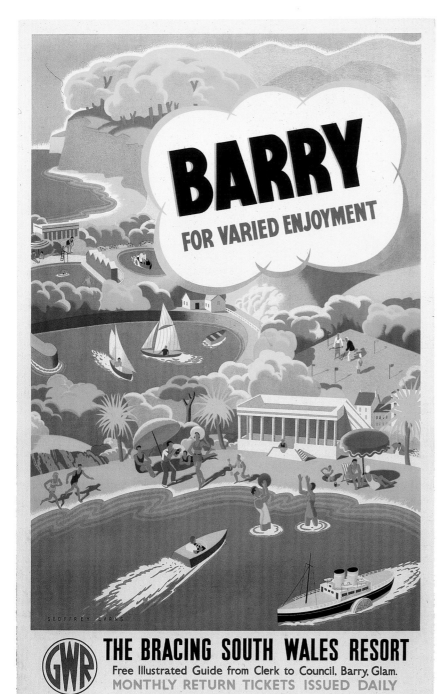

Barry for Varied Enjoyment
by Geoffrey Evans, 1937.
This poster was produced in conjunction with Barry Council to share costs and increase circulation. South Wales was promoted as a family holiday area and the 'bracing air' slogan was laboured because bracing air was considered to be good for the constitution, although it was used much earlier and more effectively by the Great Northern Railway in the posters of Skegness. The GWR offered the idea of a perfect holiday – sandy beaches, pools, pleasure boats and golf.

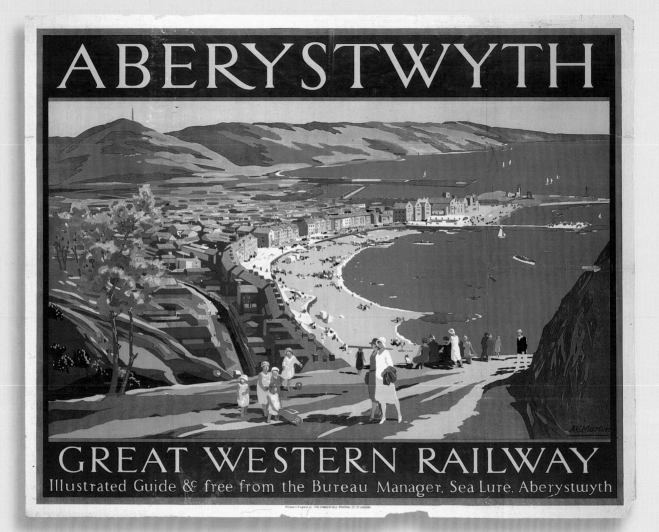

Aberystwyth by A.E. Martin, 1928

The Great Western advertised Aberystwyth as a bustling, crowded, sunny seaside town and a haunt for the fashionable. The town called itself 'The Queen of the Cambrian Coast'; situated on the northern bank of the Rheidol in the centre of Cardigan Bay, it boasted an ocean amphitheatre as well as a pier, bandstand, a town library and a high sunshine record. The booklet 'South Wales – Its Annals, Antiquities and Attractions' published in 1914 calls Aberystwyth 'The British Biarritz' and describes it as 'fashionable in 1807', 'delectable in 1837', 'progressive in 1857' and 'undeniably up-to-date in 1914'! The town council likened it to Tunbridge Wells and claimed to care for the visitor's 'mental and physical' culture.

Porthcawl.

The 1937 illustrated guide gives a comprehensive listing of the facilities available in this South Wales resort and its surroundings. 'Porthcawl's sole business is providing for the pleasure of its visitors and there are no commercial enterprises within miles to sully the shining cleanliness of the town, which is alone a sufficient proof of the exquisite purity and tonic freshness of Porthcawl air!'

PORTHCAWL
GLAMORGAN

The Gem of the Severn Sea

Quiet Retreats on the River Thames.
An unusual style of folding illustrated booklet from the 1930s
describing the route of the Thames from Iffley (near Oxford) all the way
to Staines, with principal hotels, boathouses, lockgates (with river
distances) and nearest stations.

  'Of all the golden words written about the oldest river in England, of
all the songs that have been sung about the romance of the stream
that has carried history for untold years from the Piltdown Man to the
Boat Race, very few tell you of the leisurely Thames.' (John E. Walsh)

Various aspects of the Mendips, Devon and Cornwall with details of travel facilities and 'Land Cruises' are described in these three similarly designed illustrated guides for 1934. The text also recommends the purchase of 'Somerset', 'Glorious Devon' and 'The Cornish Riviera' books for further information. All these covers came from the studios of Ralph Mott.

Summer Holiday Tickets (1931).
This leaflet listed special fares and availability of 'concession tickets' and week-end rates to many destinations, including Ireland. In the introduction the guide states: 'Whatever be the choice of the holidaymaker – seaside, moorland, the hills, or open country spaces – the ideal spot will be found in the territory served by the Great Western Railway.'

The 1932 edition of 'Summer Holiday Tickets' gave similar listings of fare options available from the stations printed on the cover to places as wide apart as Folkestone, Carlisle, the Eastern Counties and even locations in Ireland (via Fishguard, Liverpool or Holyhead).

GWR Reduced Fares (1930).
The young lady on the cover is taking full advantage of the special rates offered by the company. The small booklet provides the public with an outline of the facilities for reduced fare travel, party outings, special rates for bands and orchestras, children, anglers, and the public attending conferences and meetings (did anyone pay the normal fare?); also Private Restaurant Cars, special party saloons, circular and walking tours and dog tickets, not to mention luggage in advance and road motor vehicles for private hire.

Newquay by Alfred Lambart, 1937.

Surfing is not a new sport. Fistral Beach in Newquay is world-renowned for the original form of surfing. It faces west and has some of the best surfing conditions in Europe. A 1925 guide book spoke of Newquay's 'phenomenal dryness' and boasted of 'the highest class of modern hotel accommodation, the best golf course and exceptionally exhilarating air'. The Cornish Riviera can still be reached by train from Paddington in about six hours and the view from the train out to sea at Dawlish Warren is timeless.

Luggage label from The Cornish Riviera Express, probably one of the most famous trains on the GWR and the subject of much literature. The name was derived from a competition in 'The Railway Magazine' in 1904, with a prize of 3 guineas (£3.15), to which 1,286 entries were received!

Known affectionately as 'the Limited', departure was prompt at 10.30 am from Paddington, taking around 4 hours to reach Plymouth, with coaches being 'slipped' *en route* for Westbury, Exeter, and Taunton. The journey to Penzance was completed in 6 hours and 20 minutes.

Camping.

The popularity of the outdoor life became quickly apparent to the GWR publicity people, and in the 1930s they produced a series of annual booklets with attractive covers giving directories of camping sites and the usual details of facilities offered by the company. All the guides were issued in March or April in good time for passengers to make arrangements. The illustrations show examples from 1932 and various issues to 1939, presenting a diversity of artwork, much of which (as usual for items other than posters) remains anonymous.

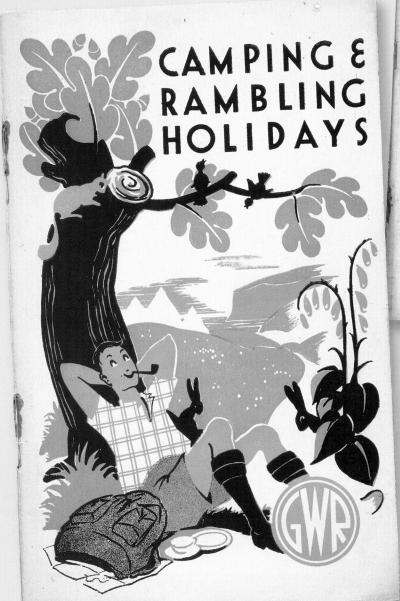

CAMPING &
RAMBLING
HOLIDAYS

GWR

camping &
rambling
holidays

GWR

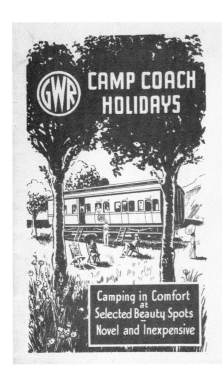

Following on from Camping & Rambling Holiday Guides the GWR converted and made available 65 older (usually clerestory) coaches that were surplus to requirements (what price the Preservation Movement?) and strategically placed them in sidings close to selected beauty spots such as Dawlish Warren (where there were nine vehicles), Marazion and Saundersfoot, with safe access, but not totally ideal for a good night's sleep as trains rumbled by!

These coaches were of 6-berth layout and were provided with oil for heating and lighting, but there were few with toilets on site, and use had to be made of the facilities at the local station. In later years during BR days, these were replaced with a number of Pullman coaches, some of which survive out of use today.

'The Hikers Mystery Express No. 2' was arranged to convey hikers from Paddington to Henley-on-Thames and every passenger was presented with a copy of the 'Chiltern Country' guide, and left to make his or her choice as to route. The train departed from Paddington at 10.45am, and returned from Henley departing at 7.02pm.

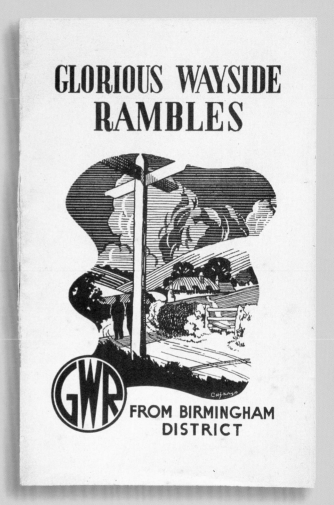

Facing page The 'Rambles' guides were all the work of Hugh E. Page between 1935 and 1939. Mr Page was a member of the North Finchley Rambling Club and was no doubt in his element whilst writing these books. He is understood to have personally checked all the information by visiting these locations and was unfortunately killed in an accident on one such walk.

His first booklet 'Rambles in the Chiltern Country' (1931) was reprinted within a month of publication and a third edition appeared in 1932. A fourth edition followed in 1937.

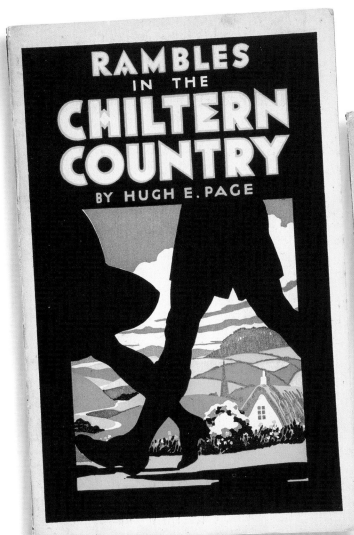

In 1932 'Rambles in South Devon' appeared and was reprinted in 1933. In rapid succession came 'Rambles in Shakespeare Land' (2 editions in 1933 and 1938), 'Rambles and Walking Tours in Somerset' (1935 and 1938), 'Rambles Around the Cambrian Coast' (1936), 'Wye Valley' (1938) and 'South Devon' (1939). Most of the latter publications subsequently carried a label warning that 'under existing conditions some of the routes may no longer be open for use by ramblers', as these editions were still available after the start of hostilities.

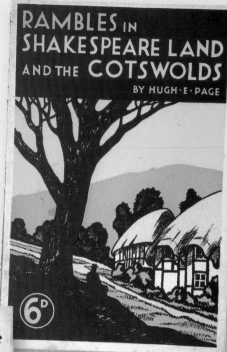

RAMBLES IN *the* WYE VALLEY

by Hugh E. Page... 6D

RAMBLES & WALKING TOURS IN SOMERSET

By Hugh E. Page

6D

RAMBLES & WALKING TOURS IN SOUTH DEVON

by HUGH E. PAGE

6D

The GWR was fortunate to have Stratford-on-Avon on its territory, probably one of the most visited places in England. The company went to great lengths to exploit its potential, and many guides were produced over the years including a number for the American market. 'The Shakespeare Country' (1937) was written by Maxwell Fraser and describes the buildings associated with the town, with added information on Warwick and Kenilworth Castles, and the towns of Leamington Spa, Rugby, and Coventry. This guide was a joint project with the LMS hence the references to towns not on the company's lines, but the LMS logo was conspicuous by its absence from the cover!

The French version from 1938 covers much the same ground and was also a joint project with the LMS. This time the latter company was represented by a logo on the back cover.

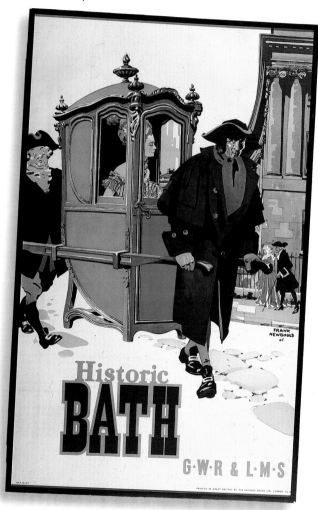

Historic Bath by Dora Batty, 1936 (*below*)

Bath advertised herself as an historic city, with references to the Roman Baths and the late eighteenth-century public buildings. These were The Pump Room, Guildhall and Assembly Rooms. Literary references were also used, and Bath was the basis for *The School for Scandal*, *The Rivals*, *Tom Jones* and much of Charles Dickens', Jane Austen's and Thomas Hardy's work. Dora Batty was a designer and illustrator for London Transport but she also taught in the Textiles Department of the Central School of Arts and Crafts.

Historic Bath by Frank Newbould, 1946

The Second World War was over and Britain looked forward to the future with hope. The railway companies wanted to get back to normal and started to advertise again to encourage passengers to travel. The posters glorified the historic grandeur of Britain and its history and traditions. Here Bath is 'historic' and characters from the seventeenth century are used to make this point. This is a joint poster produced by the GWR and LMS. Both covered this city and both would have been run down and left in financial straits after the war. Designer Frank Newbould had been attached to the War Office during the conflict.

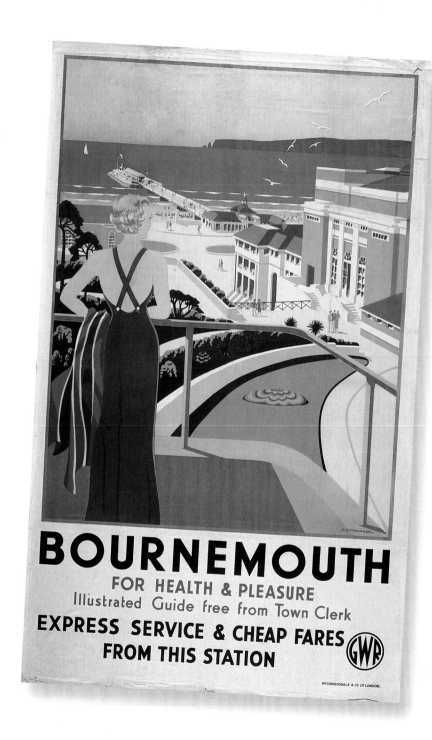

Bournemouth by G.D. Tidmarsh, *c*.1937. Bournemouth is more usually associated with the Southern Railway, but the GWR also ran into the town. Until the mid-nineteenth century Bournemouth was a little fishing village but by the late 1930s it was a recognised health resort for the fashionable.

Jersey

This guide produced in 1937 was another 'joint' production between the Southern Railway and the Great Western, who together offered a daily service via Weymouth or Southampton by twin screw and turbine steamers. Cheap facilities were offered all the year round and holders of return tickets could travel by either company's steamers on the homeward journey.

Guernsey

The 1939 season guide was again a joint production with the SR offering much the same facilities as the previous guide – the weekend fare from Paddington via Weymouth Ferry was 42s, but 'in addition to the railway company's steamer services, Guernsey may be reached by air this summer daily from London and Southampton and at weekends from Brighton and Exeter.' All very friendly co-operation!

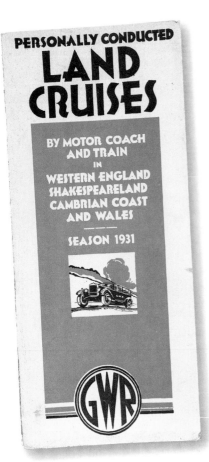

Motor Touring Arrangements (1936). This guide covered the conveyance of a car or motor-cycle by cross-channel GWR services or through the Severn Tunnel. 'Depending on the passenger ticket holding, cars may be conveyed by passenger train at the reduced rate of 1½, 2¼ or 3d per mile (at owner's risk) with a minimum 50 miles rail journey and limited to rail journeys in Great Britain only'.

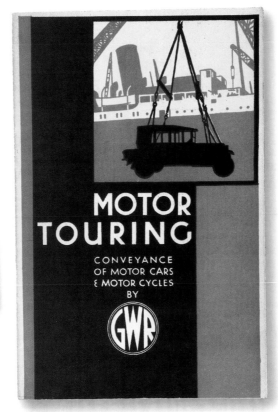

Key to Your Luggage Problem (1935) – a mini-guide giving an in depth detailed summary of the various ways of sending luggage in advance via container or alternative means.

Personally Conducted Land Cruises (1931) gave 4 different destinations including North and South Wales, Devon and Cornwall. 'Each "cruise" begins and ends with a train journey (1st class), and is taken by road in the magnificently appointed motor coaches purchased by the company expressly for these cruises. First class accommodation is reserved in advance and each tour is accompanied by a GWR representative'.

To cater for other popular activities the company produced several booklets on the subject of golf. 'Golf Courses' (1934) gave a list of courses across virtually the whole of the GWR system, with details of accommodation and green fees. Special facilities were offered for parties of four or more golfers attending matches, competitions or exhibitions for one day. Return tickets were issued at about the single fare by prior arrangement or on the surrender of a special voucher. Locations for accommodation included hotels under the management of the GWR. Fees varied, but around 15s per week was the average cost of membership. This guide appeared in various editions with several containing the Rules of Game for the inexperienced player!

Another guide – entitled 'Bowling Greens Served by the GWR' (1934) – served a similar purpose as the golf publications. This particular example had a foreword by S.W.P. Walpole (Honorary Secretary of the London and Southern Counties Bowling Association) who wrote: 'the modern level green game is fast becoming an absorbing passion with many thousands of our fellow citizens both male and female'.
The guide lists greens and clubs alphabetically, from Aberaman to Ystrad Mynach, with fees (in shillings *per annum*) for members and visitors.

GWR Air Services by Ralph & Brown, 1933.

This is the actual artwork (gouache on cardboard) for the poster. There were only 500 printed and the design company received fifteen guineas for the work. Artists and designers preferred to be paid in guineas rather than pounds as it was considered to be more respectable. Ralph & Mott was a firm of artists' agents and Ralph & Brown were probably two of the artists from this team. Some of the artists became well known in their own right in later years.

The first Great Western air service was between Cardiff and Plymouth. In 1933 the plane, crew and engineers were supplied by Imperial Airways and the Great Western supplied the traffic staff. It was the Great Western that took the lead in getting the railways off the ground. The plane was a Westland Wessex monoplane painted in the Great Western colours of Windsor Brown and White (Chocolate and Cream) with the monogram on each side of the rudder. When the plane landed at Plymouth the passengers were transferred to a bus which connected the airport with a railway station. The cost from Cardiff to Plymouth was £3 10s single and £6 return. Letters were also carried on the service for 3d above the normal postal rate. The first season resulted in a net loss, so in 1934 a plan was drawn up to establish an airline jointly owned by the four major railway companies and Imperial Airways. This became known as The Railway Air Services and ran until 1939 when the government claimed its services for the war effort. Operation eventually ground to a halt in 1947.

Illustrated are two guides from 1933 with cover designs by Charles Mayo. Example fares from Cardiff to Torquay were £3 single and £5 return with connecting buses. There were two flights a day in each direction.

Mail carried by the GWR Air Services was initially franked with a 3d black and green prepaid newspaper label from the Inaugural flight in addition to the normal letter rate of 1½d. Then on 15th May 1933 the company issued a special 3d 'GWR AIRMAIL' stamp which remained in use until the service was suspended at the end of September of that year with the project losing money. 12,000 copies were printed in sheets of thirty (six rows of five stamps). Surviving complete sheets are rare. A luggage label for the service is shown below.

Door to Door Transport by GWR, undated leaflet from the 1930s.

'The conveyance by rail of merchandise which in the usual course requires to be carefully packed has been revolutionised by the introduction of the Road-Rail Container. Goods can be loaded in containers by the sender's experts on the premises, a minimum of packing being used. Containers are available for the conveyance of all descriptions of merchandise including household removals.' The service had a certain similarity to the more sophisticated Freightliner service of today.

Exceptional Loads (1933).

A guide to specialised wagons available for the conveyance of loads of exceptional dimensions and abnormal weight and also for merchandise requiring special care in transit. Loads which at first sight were 'out of gauge' could be accommodated by special arrangements 'which permit the passage of practically any object'. Illustrated examples show a naval gun 62 feet long and weighing 108 tons, a 4-bladed ship's propeller measuring 13 feet 6 inches square, an excavator, a 23-ton granite block and an anti-aircraft gun!

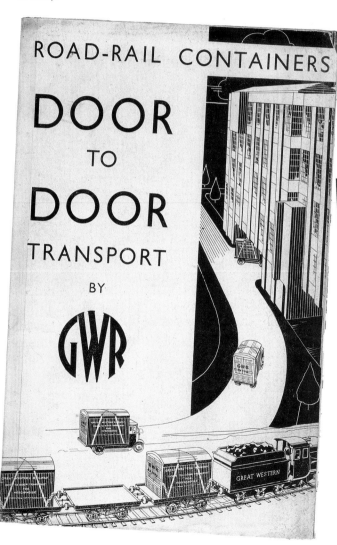

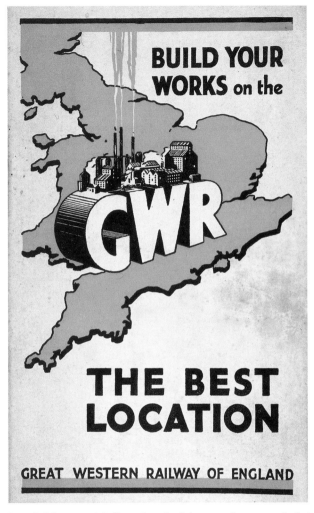

Intended for potential clients from both home and overseas, both brochures have 'GWR of England' on the cover.
The company maintained a register of factory sites adjacent to its system suitable for development and were prepared to supply photographs of various premises recently erected beside the company tracks.

'These sites possess the advantages of cheap lighting and power, ample water supply and in many instances coal and raw materials are within easy reach.'

HMV and Nestlés at Hayes, the Slough Trading Estate, Morris Motors of Cowley and Frys of Keynsham were given as examples of successful sites. 'Build Your Works' and 'Factory Sites' date from 1932 and 1936 respectively.

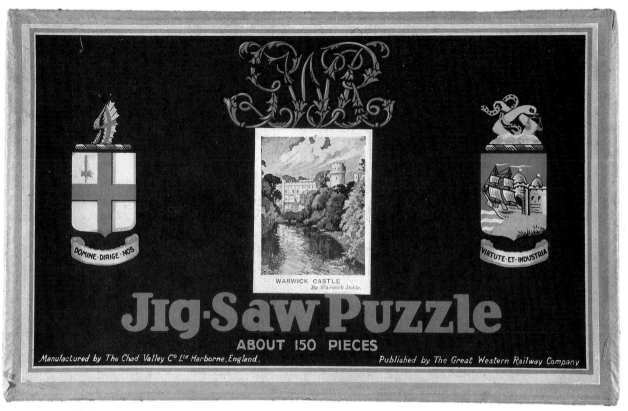

In 1924 the brand new GWR locomotive 'Caerphilly Castle' was displayed by the company at the Wembley exhibition. Felix Pole came up with the idea of having some form of souvenir on the stand for visiting children. In conjunction with the Chad Valley Co., a wooden jigsaw was produced using an illustration supplied by the publicity section, which appeared initially in a fairly plain blue box. Originally priced at 5s, it had disappointing sales, so the price was reduced to 2s 6d, resulting in no fewer than 30,000 puzzles being sold by the end of the year.

Continuing with this success, 44 different puzzles were produced up to the end of 1939, with over 1,000,000 sold. The puzzles covered railway subjects, scenic views and historic events and were available in various flat and bookshelf style boxes. Eleven titles were still listed at 2s 6d in 1939.

The puzzles were apparently sold at near cost price, the public effectively paying for the advertising and at the same time giving hours of pleasure to many recipients. The puzzle box above showing Warwick Castle was on sale between 1930 and 1933 and the illustration on the left shows 'Brazenose College' (Oxford), from a poster by Claude Buckle, which was on sale from 1933 until 1939.

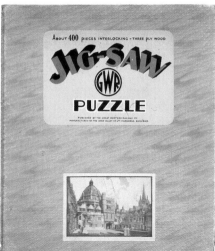

As a further experiment Chad Valley devised a board game called 'Race to the Ocean Coast' which was advertised in 'Holiday Haunts' for 1930. The game consisted of a GWR system map printed on a folding board, and was played along the lines of 'Snakes and Ladders', with two versions being produced.

It was also priced 2s 6d but unlike the jigsaws was not successful. Approximately 5,500 sets of the two versions were sold and the following year the game was withdrawn.

The GWR produced a number of publications for overseas circulation – the Canadian and American markets were handled by agencies in Toronto and New York, and several examples are known in Russian and Swedish.

A large book 'GWR Docks' was printed in English, French and German and contained a map of every dockyard served by the company. This must have been quite useful to the Luftwaffe!

The unusual 'Romantik and Erholung in England' (Romanticism and Recuperation) booklet was printed in Berlin (1930) with the entire text in German.

This concert was promoted by the GWR (London) Musical Society, augmented by the Swindon Choir and Orchestra at the Queens Hall, London, on 19th March 1937. All the performers were amateurs, apart from the soloists.

The programme consisted of music by British composers for Coronation Year, including selections from 'Merrie England', which was all very patriotic. The advertising in the programme notes was sponsored by suppliers of electrical cables, saws and steel pipes!